The following is simply a checklist for what to watch out for. You may have to look at more specific publications to find a greater discussion and more detailed analysis.

1. Obama care mandate for 2015.

Those who do not purchase health insurance during 2015 are subject to a tax penalty in 2015. The penalty amount for 2015 is increased to the lesser of 2% of your income or $325 per adult and $162.50 per dependent under age 18 living in your household. However, the penalty is capped at the national average premium, which is $207 per individual (up from $204 per individual in 2014).

2. Itemized medical expenses. For 2015, the rate for medical driving is 23 cents per mile (a half cent less than in 2014).

3. Long-term care coverage. The portion of long-term care insurance premiums that are treated as a deductible medical expense has increased slightly in 2015 for each age group.
4. Flexible spending arrangements (FSAs). In 2015, the maximum salary contribution to an FSA is limited to $2,550 (up from $2,500 in 2014).

5. Health savings accounts and Archer medical savings accounts. The contribution limits for HSAs and MSAs in 2015 have been increased slightly.
6. Accelerated death benefits. For chronically ill individuals, the daily dollar limit excludable from gross income for 2015 is $330. Amounts in excess are taxable to the extent they exceed actual long-term care costs.

7. ABLE (Achieving a Better Life Experience). It is designed to help pay costs of a person who is disabled with blindness or a disability under the Social Security Act, where a person has a disability on file with the IRS (look for further clarification in the coming months). Contributions are not tax deductible, but withdrawals to pay qualified expenses are tax free much like Disability payments. Deductible expenses are the costs for health, education, and welfare.

8. American opportunity credit. There is no modified adjusted gross income limit change in 2015 for eligibility to claim the credit
9. Lifetime learning credit. The modified adjusted gross income limits on eligibility to claim the credit have been increased slightly for 2015.

10. Tuition and fees deduction. The above-the-line deduction for tuition and fees of up to $4,000 for
2015 is not yet extended as of 12/25/2015. Based on the previous year (an also an election year coming up in 2016, the odds are this deduction will remain to get the "younger vote out".

11. Student loan interest. There is no modified adjusted gross income (magi) limit change in 2015 The deduction remains the same and unchanged.
12. Interest on U.S. savings bonds. The MAGI limits on the claim of exclusion for interest on bonds redeemed to pay higher education costs have been increased for 2015.

13. Mortgage insurance. The ability to treat mortgage insurance as deductible mortgage interest has not been determined as yet for 2015. The fallout would generate enough front page news that it is unlikely it will be removed from

the tax deductions for 2015. However, stranger things have happened when one party is trying to blame the other political party for not getting things done. Wait and see, it should be interesting. A loan modification in and of itself does not give rise to an actual interest deduction until that interest is actually paid.

14. Cancellation of mortgage debt. The foreclosure and debt forgiveness or Cancellation of a debt may still be excluded into 2015 if Congress extends the 2014 expiration. The verdict is still out if this law will be extended for 2015 or not. Currently, it appears it will.

15. Moving expenses. Use of a vehicle for deductible moving purposes in 2015 is figured at the rate of 23 cents per mile (a half cent less than in 2014).

16. Energy improvements. The residential energy property credit for adding insulation or installing energy-efficient windows and exterior doors, is up for grabs. The verdict is still out if this law will be extended for 2015 or not. Currently, it appears it will.

17. Parsonage allowance. Members of the clergy can exclude housing allowance they receive.
18. Traditional IRAs and Roth IRAs. MAGI limits on contributions have increased for 2015. There is no change to the contribution limit of $5,500 or to the "catch-up" limit of $1,000 for 50 years old by the end of 2015. It does however limit rollovers to one per taxpayer starting in 2015

19. 401(k) and similar plans. The 2015 elective deferral contribution limit and additional contribution limit for age 50 or older have been increased to $18,000 and $6,000,.
20. Self-employed retirement plans. Contribution, benefit, and other limits for these plans have been increased for 2015.
21. Simplified Employee Pension plans (SEPs). Contribution limits for these plans have been increased for 2015. Earnings threshold for including an employee in a SEP have also been increased.

22. Savings Incentive Match Plans for Employees (SIMPLEs). Contribution limit for SIMPLEs and the additional contribution limit for those age 50 or older by the end of the year 2015 are increased to $12,500 and $3,000 each.

23. Retirement saver's credit. The MAGI limits have been increased for

2015.

24. Charitable transfers of IRA distributions. The rule allowing those age 701/2 and older to transfer up to $100,000 of IRA funds directly to a public charity on a tax-free basis is still up in the air. The verdict is still out if this law will be extended for 2015 or not. Currently, it appears it will.

25. Business use of your personal car. The standard mileage ratein 2015 is 57.5¢ per mile (a penny and a half more than in 2014).
26. Business travel per diem rates. The maximum federal per diem rate for travel is $129 per day ($83 for lodging and $46 for meals).
27. Driving your car for medical or moving purposes. The IRS standard mileage rate for 2015 is 23 cents per mile.
28. Equipment purchases. Two key changes impact write-offs for equipment purchases in 2015:

First-year expensing. The $500,000 limit was extended retroactively for 2014 and unless it is extended again, the limit for the Section 179 deduction in 2015 will be $25,000 and this limit will phase out when purchases exceed $200,000.

29. Bonus depreciation. Bonus depreciation was extended for 2014. The verdict is still out if this law will be extended for 2015 or not. Currently, it appears it will. Bonus depreciation—50% deduction
30. Self-employment tax. The self-employment tax in 2015 is $118,500 (up from $117,000 in 2014).

31. Standard mileage rate. the standard mileage rate, for 2015; it is 57.5¢ cents per mile (a cent and a half more than in 2014). Those who use the standard mileage rate for 2015 must reduce the vehicle's basis by 24¢ per mile (the rate in 2014 was 22¢ per mile).
32. State and local sales taxes. Unless Congress extends the deduction of State and Local Taxes, it will expire on Dec. 31, 2014 and not be usable for your 2015 tax returns. This is a pretty widely known deduction and well used so the likelihood of not being extended seems rather remote.

33. Gifts you receive. The annual exclusion amount for 2015 is $14,000 per recipient (the same as in 2014).
34. Standard deduction amounts. The basic standard deduction amounts for 2015 have been increased for all filing statuses:

- Married filing jointly and surviving spouses: $12,600
- Heads of households: $9,250
- Singles and married filing separately: $6,300

Additional standard deduction amounts. For 2015, the additional standard deduction amount for age and/or blindness remains unchanged at $1,550 for single filers and heads of households, but for married filers (filing jointly or separately) and surviving spouses, it has increased to $1,250.

35. Earned income credit. The earned income credit amounts, including adjusted gross income limits, have been increased for 2015.
36. Educator expenses up to $250—deductible as an adjustment to gross income
37. Energy-efficient buildings—deduction up to $1.80 per square foot
38. First-year expensing—enhanced deduction
39. IRA transfers directly to charity by those age 701/2—tax free up to $100,000

It has long been established that the Internal Revenue does not necessarily follow court decisions that are more favorable to the taxpayer. They sometimes take the approach that until a higher court, more specifically a District Court of Appeals or the Supreme Court rules on the matter, the Service will take a more favorable position that more adequately reflects their interpretation of the law. Again, this in interpretation and not law. There has been and will continue to be an enormous amount of litigation concerning the rights of a taxpayer for representation in front of the IRS. The right of representation has several thousand years of precedence going all the way back to any citizen could have it's Senator represent him in a Roman Quorum. The following discourse is the official position of the IRS and not that of the courts. In too many cases to list, the opposite position has prevailed. Caution would be the best rules to follow in the following discussions;
What's New

Representative designations. IRS no longer recognizes the registered tax return preparer designation. All unenrolled return preparers must provide a valid PTIN to represent a taxpayer before the IRS. For returns prepared after December 31, 2015, only unenrolled return preparers participating in the

Annual Filing Season Record of Completion program may represent a taxpayer, and only with respect to returns prepared and signed by the preparer.

Representative signatures. Form 2848 now provides space for the information and signatures of up to four representatives. For more information, see the instructions to Form 2848, Line 2. Representatives(s).

Revisions to Circular 230. Amendments to Circular 230 (Rev. 6-2015), the rules governing practice before the IRS, include recent noteworthy changes.

• Practitioner's written tax advice. Requirements for certain written tax opinions (known as "covered opinions") were replaced with principles-based requirements applicable to all practitioners' written tax advice.

• Practitioner's general competency requirement. A general competency requirement, under which a practitioner must have or obtain the knowledge, skill, thoroughness, and preparation necessary for whatever matter the practitioner has undertaken for a client has been added to Circular 230.

• Negotiation of taxpayer checks. The explicit recognition that a longstanding prohibition in Circular 230 against negotiation of Treasury "checks" issued to taxpayers likewise applies to direct deposits and similar electronic forms of payment that are now commonplace. See Negotiation of taxpayer refund checks , under What Are the Rules of Practice?, later.

• Suspension from practice. Circular 230 expands and refines the process for suspension from practice on an expedited basis, which allows the Office of Professional Responsibility to promptly suspend individuals in certain situations using a short form of administrative due process.

For further information see Circular 230 (Rev. 6-2015), Regulations Governing Practice before the Internal Revenue Service.

Annual Filing Season Program and Directory of Federal Tax Return Preparers. The IRS has developed an online searchable database of tax return preparers who participate in the Annual Filing Season Program. The general public can access the database on the IRS website. The IRS developed the directory as part of the Annual Filing Season Program. For further information see below, Annual Filing Season Program .

Introduction

This . discusses who may represent a taxpayer before the IRS and what forms
or documents are used to authorize a person to represent a taxpayer. Usually,
attorneys, certified public accountants (CPAs), and enrolled agents may
represent taxpayers before the IRS. Enrolled retirement plan agents, and
enrolled actuaries may represent with respect to specified Internal Revenue
Code sections delineated in Circular 230. Under special and limited
circumstances, other individuals, including unenrolled return preparers,
family members, employees, and students can represent taxpayers before the
IRS. For details regarding taxpayer representation, see Who Can Practice
Before the IRS? , later.

Definitions. Many of the terms used in this ., such as "enrolled agent" and
"practitioner" are defined in the Glossary at the back of this ..

Table of Contents

Practice Before the IRS

The Office of Professional Responsibility generally has responsibility for
matters related to practitioner conduct, and exclusive responsibility for
discipline, including disciplinary proceedings and sanctions. The Return
Preparer Office is responsible for matters related to the issuance of PTINs,
acting on applications for enrollment and administering competency testing
and continuing education for designated groups.

What Is Practice Before the IRS? Circular 230 covers all matters relating to any of the following.
• Communicating with the IRS on behalf of a taxpayer regarding the taxpayer's rights, privileges, or liabilities under laws and regulations administered by the IRS.
• Representing a taxpayer at conferences, hearings, or meetings with the IRS.
• Preparing, filing or submitting documents, or advising on the preparation, filing or submission of documents, including tax returns, with the IRS on behalf of a taxpayer.
• Providing a client with written tax advice on one or more Federal matters.

Any individual may for compensation prepare or assist with the preparation of a tax return or claim for refund, appear as a witness for the taxpayer before the IRS, or furnish information at the request of the IRS or any of its officers or employees.

Who Can Practice Before the IRS?

The following individuals are subject to the Regulations contained in Circular 230. However, any individual who is authorized generally to practice (a recognized representative) must be designated as the taxpayer's representative and file a written declaration with the IRS stating that he or she is authorized and qualified to represent a particular taxpayer. Form 2848 can be used for this purpose.

Appraisers. Any individual who prepares appraisals supporting the valuation of assets in connection with one or more federal tax matters is subject to the regulations contained in Circular 230. Appraisers have no representation rights but may appear as witnesses on behalf of taxpayers.

Attorneys. Any attorney who is not currently under suspension or disbarment from practice before the IRS and who is a member in good standing of the bar of the highest court of any state, possession, territory, commonwealth, or the District of Columbia may practice before the IRS.

Certified public accountants (CPAs). Any CPA who is not currently under suspension or disbarment from practice before the IRS and who is duly qualified to practice as a CPA in any state, possession, territory, commonwealth, or the District of Columbia may practice before the IRS.

Enrolled agents. Any enrolled agent in active status who is not currently under suspension or disbarment from practice before the IRS may practice before the IRS.

Enrolled retirement plan agents. Any enrolled retirement plan agent in active status who is not currently under suspension or disbarment from practice before the IRS may practice before the IRS. The practice of enrolled retirement plan agents is limited to certain Internal Revenue Code sections that relate to their area of expertise, principally those sections governing employee retirement plans.

Enrolled actuaries. Any individual who is enrolled as an actuary by the Joint Board for the Enrollment of Actuaries who is not currently under suspension or disbarment from practice before the IRS may practice before the IRS. The practice of enrolled actuaries is limited to certain Internal Revenue Code sections that relate to their area of expertise, principally those sections governing employee retirement plans.

Low Income Taxpayer Clinic Student Interns. Under certain circumstances, a student who is supervised by a practitioner at a law school or equivalent program providing tax services for low income taxpayers may request authorization to represent a taxpayer before the IRS. For more information, see Authorization for Special Appearances , later.

Unenrolled return preparers. An unenrolled return preparer is an individual other than an attorney, CPA, enrolled agent, enrolled retirement plan agent, or enrolled actuary who prepares and signs a taxpayer's return as the paid preparer, or who prepares a return but is not required (by the instructions to the return or regulations) to sign the return.

Unenrolled return preparers may represent taxpayers only before revenue agents, customer service representatives, or similar officers and employees of the Internal Revenue Service (including the Taxpayer Advocate Service) and only during an examination of the tax returns they prepared and signed prior to December 31, 2015. Unenrolled return preparers may not represent taxpayers before appeals officers, revenue officers, counsel or similar officers or employees of the Internal Revenue Service or the Department of Treasury. Unenrolled return preparers may not execute closing agreements, extend the statutory period for tax assessments or collection of tax, execute waivers, or sign any document on behalf of a taxpayer.

If an unenrolled return preparer does not meet the requirements for limited representation, you may authorize the unenrolled return preparer to inspect and/or request your tax information by filing Form 8821. Completing Form 8821 will not authorize the unenrolled return preparer to represent you before the IRS. See Form 8821.

Annual Filing Season Program Record of Completion. Beginning January 1, 2016, only unenrolled return preparers who hold a record of completion for BOTH the tax return year (2015 or thereafter) under examination and the year the examination is conducted may represent under the following conditions: Unenrolled return preparers may represent taxpayers only before revenue agents, customer service representatives, or similar officers and employees of the Internal Revenue Service (including the Taxpayer Advocate Service) and only during an examination of the taxable year or period covered by the tax returns they prepared and signed. Unenrolled return preparers may not represent taxpayers, regardless of the circumstances requiring representation, before appeals officers, revenue officers, counsel or similar officers or employees of the Internal Revenue Service or the Department of Treasury. Unenrolled return preparers may not execute closing agreements, extend the statutory period for tax assessments or collection of tax, execute waivers, or sign any document on behalf of a taxpayer.

If an unenrolled return preparer does not meet the requirements for limited representation, you may authorize the unenrolled return preparer to inspect and/or request your tax information by filing Form 8821. Completing Form 8821 will not authorize the unenrolled return preparer to represent you before any IRS personnel. See Form 8821.
Practice denied. Any individual engaged in limited practice before the IRS who is involved in disreputable conduct is subject to disciplinary action. Disreputable conduct includes, but is not limited to, the list of items under Incompetence and Disreputable Conduct shown later under What Are the Rules of Practice? .

Other individuals who may serve as representatives. Because of their special relationship with a taxpayer, the following individuals may represent the specified taxpayers before the IRS, provided they present satisfactory identification and, except in the case of an individual described in (1) below, proof of authority to represent the taxpayer.

1. An individual. An individual can represent himself or herself before the IRS and does not have to file a written declaration of qualification and authority.
2. A family member. An individual can represent members of his or her immediate family. Immediate family includes a spouse, child, parent, brother, or sister of the individual.

3. An officer. A bona fide officer of a corporation (including a parent, subsidiary, or other affiliated corporation), association, or organized group can represent the corporation, association, or organized group. An officer of a governmental unit, agency, or authority, in the course of his or her official duties, can represent the organization before the IRS.

4. A partner. A general partner may represent the partnership before the IRS.

5. An employee. A regular full-time employee can represent his or her employer. An employer can be, but is not limited to, an individual, partnership, corporation (including a parent, subsidiary, or other affiliated corporation), association, trust, receivership, guardianship, estate, organized group, governmental unit, agency, or authority.

6. A fiduciary. A fiduciary (trustee, executor, personal representative, administrator, receiver, or guardian) stands in the position of a taxpayer and acts as the taxpayer, not as a representative. See Fiduciary under When Is a Power of Attorney Not Required? , later.

Representation Outside the United States

Any individual may represent an individual or entity, who is outside the United States, before personnel of the IRS when such representation also occurs outside the United States. See section 10.7(c)(1)(vii) of Circular 230.

Authorization for Special Appearances

The Commissioner of Internal Revenue, or delegate, can authorize an individual who is not otherwise eligible to practice before the IRS to represent another person for a particular matter. The prospective representative must request this authorization in writing from the Office of Professional Responsibility. However, it is granted only when extremely compelling circumstances exist. If granted, the Commissioner, or delegate, will issue a letter that details the conditions related to the appearance and the particular tax matter for which the authorization is granted.

The authorization letter should not be confused with a letter from an IRS center advising an individual that he or she has been assigned a Centralized Authorization File (CAF) number. The issuance of a CAF number does not indicate that an individual is either recognized or authorized to practice before the IRS. It merely confirms that a centralized file for authorizations has been established for the individual under that number.

Students in LITCs and the STCP. A student who works in a Low Income Taxpayer Clinic (LITC) or a Student Tax Clinic Program (STCP) must receive permission to represent taxpayers before the IRS by virtue of their status as a law, business, or accounting student. Authorization requests must be sent to the Taxpayer Advocate Service. If granted, a letter authorizing the student's special appearance and detailing any conditions related to the appearance will be issued. Students receiving an authorization letter generally can represent taxpayers before any IRS function or office subject to any conditions in the authorization letter and must be under the direct supervision of an individual authorized to practice before the IRS. If you intend to have a student represent you, review the authorization letter and ask your student, your student's supervisor, or the Taxpayer Advocate Service if you have questions about the terms of the authorization.

Who May Not Practice Before the IRS?

In general, individuals who are not eligible, or who have lost the privilege as a result of certain actions, may not practice before the IRS. If an individual loses eligibility to practice, the IRS will not recognize a power of attorney that names the individual as a representative.

Corporations, associations, partnerships, and other persons that are not individuals. These organizations (or persons) are not eligible to practice before the IRS.
Loss of Eligibility
Generally, individuals lose their eligibility to practice before the IRS in the following ways.
• Not meeting the requirements for renewal of enrollment (such as continuing

professional education).

• Requesting to be placed in inactive retirement status.

• Being suspended or disbarred, or determined ineligible for practice, by the Office of Professional Responsibility for violating the regulations contained in Circular 230 or the standards in Revenue Procedure 81–38.

• Losing their state license to practice as an attorney or a certified public accountant, irrespective of the basis for the license revocation.

Failure to meet requirements. Enrolled individuals and Record of Completion holders who fail to comply with the requirements for eligibility for renewal will be notified by the IRS. The notice will explain the reason for ineligibility and provide the individual with a time-sensitive opportunity to furnish information for reconsideration.

Inactive roster. An enrolled individual will be placed on the roster of inactive enrolled individuals for a period of three years, if he or she:

• Fails to respond timely to the notice of noncompliance with the renewal requirements,

• Fails to file timely the application for renewal, or

• Does not satisfy the requirements of eligibility for renewal.

The enrolled individual must file an application for renewal and satisfy all requirements for renewal after being placed in inactive status. Otherwise, at the conclusion of the next renewal cycle, he or she will be removed from the roster and the enrollment status will be terminated.

Inactive retirement status. Enrolled individuals who request to be placed in an inactive retirement status will be ineligible to practice before the IRS. They must continue to adhere to all renewal requirements. They can be reinstated to active enrollment status by filing an application for renewal and providing evidence that they have completed the required continuing professional education hours for the enrollment cycle or registration year.

Suspension and disbarment. All individuals practicing before the IRS are subject to disciplinary proceedings and may be censured, suspended, disbarred or monetarily penalized for violating any regulation in Circular 230. This includes engaging in acts demonstrating incompetence or disreputable conduct. For more information, see Incompetence and Disreputable Conduct under What Are the Rules of Practice? , later.

Practitioners who are suspended or disbarred in a disciplinary proceeding are not allowed to represent taxpayers before the IRS during the period of suspension/disbarment. A practitioner can seek reinstatement from the Office of Professional Responsibility at the earlier of a specified period of suspension or after five years of disbarment. See What Is Practice Before the IRS? , earlier.

If the practitioner seeks reinstatement, he or she may not practice before the IRS until the Office of Professional Responsibility grants reinstatement. The Office of Professional Responsibility may reinstate the practitioner:

• If the practitioner's future conduct is not likely to be in violation of the regulations, and
• If granting the reinstatement would not be contrary to the public interest.
• Subject to other conditions for a reasonable period.

How Does an Individual Become Enrolled? The IRS website www.irs.gov/Tax-Professionals/Enrolled-Agents/Become-an-Enrolled-Agent provides complete information on the steps to be taken to become an enrolled agent.

For complete rules on earning an Annual Filing Season Program Record of Completion, see www.irs.gov/Tax-Professionals/Annual-Filing-Season-Program.
What Are the Rules of Practice?

The rules governing practice before the IRS are published in the Code of Federal Regulations at 31 C.F.R. Subtitle A, Part 10 and released digitally as Treasury Department Circular No. 230 (Circular 230). The regulations can be accessed at www.irs.gov/Tax-Professionals/Circular-230-Tax-Professionals. An attorney, CPA, enrolled agent, enrolled retirement plan agent, or enrolled actuary authorized to practice before the IRS (referred to hereafter as a practitioner) and an appraiser has the duty to perform certain acts and is restricted from performing other acts. In addition, a practitioner cannot engage in disreputable conduct (discussed later). Any practitioner who does not comply with the rules of practice or who engages in incompetent or disreputable conduct is subject to disciplinary action. Also, unenrolled preparers must comply with the rules of practice and conduct to exercise the privilege of limited practice before the IRS. There are two specific sets of rules that apply, both are contained in Circular 230:

1. Duties and Restrictions relating to practice (Subpart B of Cir. 230), and
2. Conduct considered to exhibit incompetence or disrepute (Subpart C, Section 10.51 of Cir. 230).
Duties and Restrictions

Individuals subject to Circular 230 must promptly submit records or information sought by a proper and lawful request from officers or employees of the IRS, except when the practitioner believes on reasonable belief and good faith that the information is privileged. Communications with respect to tax advice between a federally authorized tax practitioner (See Internal Revenue Code (IRC) sec. 7525) and a taxpayer generally are confidential to the same extent that communication would be privileged if it were between a taxpayer and an attorney if the advice relates to:

• Noncriminal tax matters before the IRS, or
• Noncriminal tax proceedings brought in federal court by or against the United States.

Communications regarding corporate tax shelters. This protection of tax advice communications does not apply to any written communications between a federally authorized tax practitioner and any person, including a director, shareholder, officer, employee, agent, or representative of a corporation if the communication involves the promotion of the direct or indirect participation of the corporation in any tax shelter.

Duty to advise. Individuals subject to Circular 230 who know that his or her client has not complied with the revenue laws or has made an error or omission in any return, document, affidavit, or other required paper, has the responsibility to advise the client promptly of the noncompliance, error, or omission, and the consequences of the noncompliance, error, or omission.

General due diligence. Individuals subject to Circular 230 must exercise due diligence when performing the following duties.
• Preparing or assisting in the preparing, approving, and filing of returns, documents, affidavits, and other papers relating to IRS matters.
• Determining the correctness of oral or written representations made by him or her to the Department of the Treasury.
• Determining the correctness of oral or written representations made by him

or her to clients with reference to any matter administered by the IRS.

Reliance on others. A presumption that due diligence has been exercised will apply in situations where there has been reliance on the work product of another person reasonable care was used in engaging, supervising, training, and evaluating the person, taking proper account of the nature of the relationship between the Circular 230 individual and the person.

Delays. Individuals subject to Circular 230 must not unreasonably delay the prompt disposition of any matter before the IRS.
Assistance from disbarred or suspended persons and former IRS employees. Individuals subject to Circular 230 must not knowingly, directly or indirectly, do the following.
• Accept assistance from, or assist, any person who is under disbarment or suspension from practice before the IRS if the assistance relates to matters considered practice before the IRS.
• Accept assistance from any former government employee where provisions of Circular 230 or any federal law would be violated.

Performance as a notary. Individuals subject to Circular 230 may not take acknowledgments, administer oaths, certify papers, or perform any official act as a notary public with respect to any matter administered by the IRS and for which he or she is employed as counsel, attorney, or agent, or in which he or she may be in any way interested.

Negotiation of taxpayer refund checks. Individuals subject to Circular 230 may not endorse or otherwise negotiate any check (including directing or accepting payment by any means, electronic or otherwise, into an account owned or controlled by the practitioner or any firm or other entity with whom the practitioner is associated) issued to a client by the government in respect of a Federal tax liability.

Incompetence and Disreputable Conduct Individuals subject to Circular 230 may be disbarred or suspended from practice before the IRS, or censured, for incompetence or disreputable conduct. A monetary penalty may also be imposed, in addition to any other discipline, on both individuals and their firms. The following list contains examples of conduct that is considered disreputable. Further examples are shown in Circular 230, Sec. 10.51(a).

• Being convicted of any criminal offense under the revenue laws or of any

offense involving dishonesty or breach of trust.
• Knowingly giving false or misleading information in connection with federal tax matters, or participating in such activity.
• Soliciting employment by prohibited means as discussed in section 10.30 of Circular 230.
• Willfully failing to file a federal tax return, evading or attempting to evade any federal tax or payment, or participating in such actions.
• Misappropriating, or failing to properly and promptly remit, funds received from clients for payment of taxes or other obligations due the United States.
• Directly or indirectly attempting to influence the official action of IRS employees by the use of threats, false accusations, duress, or coercion, or by offering gifts, favors, or any special inducements.

• Being disbarred or suspended from practice as an attorney, CPA, public accountant, or actuary, by the District of Columbia or any state, possession, territory, commonwealth, or any federal court, or any federal agency, body, or board.

• Knowingly aiding and abetting another person to practice before the IRS during a period of suspension, disbarment, or ineligibility of that other person.

• Using abusive language, making false accusations and statements knowing them to be false, circulating or publishing malicious or libelous matter, or engaging in any contemptuous conduct in connection with practice before the IRS.

• Giving a false opinion knowingly, recklessly, or through gross incompetence; or following a pattern of providing incompetent opinions in questions arising under the federal tax laws.
Censure, Disbarments, and Suspensions

The Secretary of the Treasury, or delegate, after notice and an opportunity for a proceeding, may censure, suspend, or disbar an individual subject to Circular 230 from practice before the IRS if the individual is shown to be incompetent or disreputable, fails to comply with the regulations in Subpart B; or with intent to defraud, willfully and knowingly misleads or threatens a client or prospective client.

Censure is a public reprimand. Individuals subject to Circular 230 include any attorney, certified public accountant, or appraiser engaged in taxpayer representation or advice-giving activity with respect to federal tax matters, enrolled agent, enrolled actuary, enrolled retirement plan agent, or annual filing season program record of completion holders.

Authorizing a Representative

You may either represent yourself, or you may authorize an individual to represent you before the IRS. If you chose to have someone represent you, your representative must be a person eligible to do so before the IRS. See Who Can Practice Before the IRS? , earlier.

What Is a Power of Attorney?

A power of attorney is your written authorization for an individual to receive your confidential tax information from the IRS and to perform certain actions on your behalf. If the authorization is not limited, the individual generally can perform all acts that you can perform, except negotiating a check. The authority granted to enrolled retirement plan agents, enrolled actuaries and unenrolled return preparers holding records of completion is limited. For information on the limits regarding annual filing season program record of completion holders, see Revenue Procedure 2015–42 and www.irs.gov/TaxProfessionals/Return-Preparer-Office-(RPO)-At-a-Glance.

Acts performed. Attorneys, certified public accountants, and enrolled agents may perform the following acts:
1. Represent you before any office of the IRS.
2. Sign an offer or a waiver of restriction on assessment or collection of a tax deficiency, or a waiver of notice of disallowance of claim for credit or refund.
3. Sign a consent to extend the statutory time period for assessment or collection of a tax.
4. Sign a closing agreement.
Signing your return. The representative named under a power of attorney is not permitted to sign your income tax return unless:
1. The signature is permitted under the Internal Revenue Code and the related regulations (see Regulations section 1.6012-1(a)(5)), and
2. You specifically authorize this in your power of attorney.
For example, the regulation permits a representative to sign your return if you are unable to sign the return due to:

• Disease or injury.

• Continuous absence from the United States (including Puerto Rico) for a period of at least 60 days prior to the date required by law for filing the return.
• Other good cause if specific permission is requested of and granted by the IRS.

When a return is signed by a representative, it must be accompanied by a power of attorney (or copy) authorizing the representative to sign the return. For more information, see the Form 2848 instructions.

Limitation on substitution or delegation. A recognized representative can substitute or delegate authority under the power of attorney to another recognized representative only if the act is specifically authorized by you on the power of attorney.

After a substitution has been made, only the newly recognized representative will be recognized as the taxpayer's representative. If a delegation of power has been made, both the original and the delegated representative will be recognized by the IRS to represent you.

Disclosure of returns to a third party. Your representative cannot execute consents that will allow the IRS to disclose tax return or return information to a third party unless you specifically delegate this authority to your representative on line 5 of Form 2848.

Incapacity or incompetency. A power of attorney is generally terminated if you become incapacitated or incompetent.

The power of attorney can continue, however, in the case of your incapacity or incompetency if you authorize this on line 5 "Other" of the Form 2848 and if your non-IRS durable power of attorney meets all the requirements for acceptance by the IRS. See Non-IRS powers of attorney , later.

When Is a Power of Attorney Required?

Submit a power of attorney when you want to authorize an individual to receive your confidential tax information and represent you before the IRS, whether or not the representative performs any of the other acts cited earlier under What Is a Power of Attorney? .

A power of attorney is most often required when you want to authorize another individual to perform at least one of the following acts on your behalf.
1. Represent you at a meeting with the IRS.
2. Prepare and file a written response to an IRS inquiry.
Form Required

Use IRS Form 2848 to appoint a recognized representative to act on your behalf before the IRS. Individuals recognized to represent you before the IRS are listed under Part II, Declaration of Representative, of Form 2848. Your representative must complete that part of the form.

Non-IRS powers of attorney. The IRS will accept a non-IRS power of attorney, but a completed Form 2848 must be attached in order for the power of attorney to be entered on the Centralized Authorization File (CAF) system. For more information, see Processing a non-IRS power of attorney , later.

If you want to use a document other than Form 2848 to authorize the representation, it must contain the following information.
• Your name and mailing address.
• Your social security number and/or employer identification number.
• Your employee plan number, if applicable.
• The name and mailing address of your representative(s).
• The types of tax involved.
• The federal tax form number.
• The specific year(s) or period(s) involved.
• For estate tax matters, the decedent's date of death.
• A clear expression of your intention concerning the scope of authority granted to your representative(s).
• Your signature and date.

You also must attach to the non-IRS power of attorney a signed and dated statement made by your representative. This statement, which is referred to as the Declaration of Representative, is contained in Part II of Form 2848. The statement should read:

1. I am not currently under suspension or disbarment from practice before the Internal Revenue Service or other practice of my profession by any other authority,

2. I am subject to regulations contained in Circular 230 (31 C.F.R., Subtitle A, Part 10) as amended, governing practice before the Internal Revenue Service,
3. I am authorized to represent the taxpayer(s) identified in the power of attorney, and
4. I am a (naming the capacity in which representation is undertaken, as set forth in the list of eligible representatives at Part II of Form 2848.)

Required information missing. The IRS will not accept your non-IRS power of attorney if it does not contain all the information listed above. You can sign and submit a completed Form 2848 or a new nonIRS power of attorney that contains all the information. If you cannot sign an acceptable replacement document, your attorney-in-fact may be able to perfect (make acceptable to the IRS) your non-IRS power of attorney by using the procedure described next.

Procedure for perfecting a non-IRS power of attorney. Under the following conditions, the attorney-infact named in your non-IRS power of attorney can sign a Form 2848 on your behalf. 1. The original non-IRS power of attorney grants authority to handle federal tax matters (for example, general authority to perform any acts).

2. The attorney-in-fact attaches a statement (signed under penalty of perjury) to the Form 2848 stating that the original non-IRS power of attorney is valid under the laws of the governing jurisdiction.
Example.

John Elm, a taxpayer, signs a non-IRS durable power of attorney that names his neighbor and CPA, Ed Larch, as his attorney-in-fact. The power of attorney grants Ed the authority to perform any and all acts on John's behalf. However, it does not list specific tax-related information such as types of tax or tax form numbers.

Shortly after John signs the power of attorney, he is declared incompetent. Later, a federal tax matter arises concerning a prior year return filed by John. Ed attempts to represent John before the IRS but is rejected because the durable power of attorney does not contain required information.

If Ed attaches a statement (signed under the penalty of perjury) that the durable power of attorney is valid under the laws of the governing jurisdiction, he can sign a completed Form 2848 and submit it on John's behalf. If Ed can practice before the IRS (see Who Can Practice Before the IRS? , earlier), he can name himself as representative on Form 2848. Otherwise, he must name another individual who can practice before the IRS.

Processing a non-IRS power of attorney. The IRS has a centralized computer database system called the CAF system. This system contains information on the authority of taxpayer representatives. Generally, when you submit a power of attorney document to the IRS, it is processed for inclusion on the CAF system. Entry of your power of attorney on the CAF system enables IRS personnel, who do not have a copy of your power of attorney, to verify the authority of your representative by accessing the CAF. It also enables the IRS to automatically send copies of notices and other IRS communications to your representative if you specify that your representative should receive those communications.

You can have your non-IRS power of attorney entered on the CAF system by attaching it to a completed Form 2848 and submitting it to the IRS. Your signature is not required; however, your attorney-in-fact must sign the Declaration of Representative (see Part II of Form 2848).

Preparation of Form — Helpful Hints
The preparation of Form 2848 is illustrated by an example, later under How Do I Fill Out Form 2848? . However, the following will also assist you in preparing the form.

Line-by-line hints. The following hints are summaries of some of the line-by-line instructions for Form 2848.
Line 1—Taxpayer information. If a joint return is involved, the husband and wife each must file a separate Form 2848 if they both want to be represented, even if the representative is the same person. If only one spouse wants to be represented in the matter, that spouse files a Form 2848.

Line 2—Representative(s). Only individuals may be named as representatives. If your representative has not been assigned a CAF number, enter "None" on that line and the IRS will issue one to your representative. If the representative's address or phone number has changed since the CAF number was issued, you should check the appropriate box. Enter your representative's fax number if available.

If you want to name more than four representatives, attach additional Form(s) 2848. The IRS will send copies of notices and communications to up to two of your representatives. You must, however, check the boxes on line 2 of the Form 2848 if you want the IRS to routinely send copies of notices and communications to your representatives. If you do not check the boxes, your representatives will not routinely receive copies of notices and communications.

Line 3—Tax matters. You may list any tax years or periods that have already ended as of the date you sign the power of attorney. You also may include on a power of attorney future tax periods if that seems appropriate under the circumstances. Avoid general references such as "all years," "all periods," or "all taxes." Any Form 2848 with such general references will be returned.

Line 4—Specific use not recorded on Centralized Authorization File (CAF). Certain matters cannot be recorded on the CAF system. Examples of such matters include, but are not limited to, the following. (A more detailed list appears in the Form 2848 instructions.)

• Requests for a private letter ruling or technical advice.
• Applications for an employer identification number (EIN).
• Claims filed on Form 843, Claim for Refund and Request for Abatement.
• Corporate dissolutions.
• Requests for change of accounting method.
• Requests for change of accounting period.
• Applications for recognition of exemption under sections 501(c)(3), 501(a), or 521 (Forms 1023, 1024, or 1028).
• Request for a determination of the qualified status of an employee benefit plan (Forms 5300, 5307, or 5310).
• Application for Award for Original Information under section 7623.
• Voluntary submissions under the Employee Plans Compliance Resolution System (EPCRS).

• Freedom of Information Act requests. If the tax matter described on line 3 of Form 2848 concerns one of these matters specifically, check the box on line 4. If this box is checked, the representative should mail or fax the power of attorney to the IRS office handling the matter. Otherwise, the representative should bring a copy of the power of attorney to each meeting with the IRS.

Where To File a Power of Attorney

Generally, you can mail or fax a paper Form 2848 directly to the IRS. To determine where you should file Form 2848, see Where To File in the instructions for Form 2848.

If Form 2848 is for a specific use, mail or fax it to the office handling that matter. For more information on specific use, see the Instructions for Form 2848, line 4.

FAX copies. The IRS will accept a copy of a power of attorney that is submitted by facsimile transmission (fax). If you choose to file a power of attorney by fax, be sure the appropriate IRS office is equipped to accept this type of transmission.

Your representative may be able to file Form 2848 electronically via the IRS website. For more information, your representative can go to www.irs.gov and under the Tax Professionals tab, click on eservices–Online Tools for Tax Professionals. If you complete Form 2848 for electronic signature authorization, do not file Form 2848 with the IRS. Instead, give it to your representative, who will retain the document.

Updating a power of attorney. Submit any update or modification to an existing power of attorney in writing. Your signature (or the signature of the individual(s) authorized to sign on your behalf) is required. Do this by sending the updated Form 2848 or non-IRS power of attorney to the IRS office(s) where you previously sent the original(s), including the center where the related return was, or will be filed.

A recognized representative may substitute or delegate authority if you specifically authorize your representative to substitute or delegate representation in the original power of attorney. To make a substitution or delegation, the representative must file the following items with the IRS office(s) where the power of attorney was filed.

1. A written notice of substitution or delegation signed by the recognized representative.

2. A written declaration of representative made by the new representative.

3. A copy of the power of attorney that specifically authorizes the substitution or delegation.

Retention/Revocation of Prior Power(s) of Attorney

A newly filed power of attorney concerning the same matter will revoke a previously filed power of attorney. However, the new power of attorney will not revoke the prior power of attorney if it specifically states it does not revoke such prior power of attorney and either of the following are attached to the new power of attorney.

• A copy of the unrevoked prior power of attorney, or
• A statement signed by the taxpayer listing the name and address of each representative authorized under the prior unrevoked power of attorney.
Note.
The filing of Form 2848 will not revoke any
Form 8821 that is in effect.
Revocation of Power of Attorney/Withdrawal of Representative

Revocation by taxpayer. If you want to revoke a previously executed power of attorney and do not want to name a new representative, you must write "REVOKE" across the top of the first page of the Form 2848 with a current signature and date immediately below this annotation. Then, you must mail or fax a copy of the power of attorney with the revocation annotation to the IRS, using the Where To File Chart, in the 2848 instructions, or if the power of attorney is for a specific matter, to the IRS office handling the matter.

Withdrawal by representative. If your representative wants to withdraw from representation, he or she must write "WITHDRAW" across the top of the first page of the Form 2848 with a current signature and date immediately below the annotation. Then, he or she must provide a copy of the power of attorney with the withdrawal annotation to the IRS in the same manner described in Revocation by taxpayer , above. If your representative does not have a copy of the power of attorney he or she wants to withdraw, he or she must send the IRS a statement of withdrawal that indicates the authority of the power of attorney is withdrawn, lists the matters and years/periods, and lists the name, TIN, and address (if known) of the taxpayer. The representative must sign and date this statement.

A power of attorney held by a student will be recorded on the CAF system for 130 days from the receipt date. If you are authorizing a student to represent you after that time, you will need to submit another updated Form 2848.

When Is a Power of Attorney Not Required?
A power of attorney is not required when the third party is not dealing with the IRS as your representative. The following situations do not require a power of attorney.
• Providing information to the IRS.

• Authorizing the disclosure of tax return information using Form 8821, Tax Information Authorization, or other written or oral disclosure consent.
• Allowing the IRS to discuss return information with a third party via the checkbox provided on a tax return or other document.

• Allowing a tax matters partner (TMP) to perform acts for the partnership.
• Allowing the IRS to discuss return information with a fiduciary.
How Do I Fill Out Form 2848?
The following example illustrates how to complete Form 2848. The two completed forms for this example are shown on the next pages.
Example.

Stan and Mary Doe have been notified that their joint tax returns (Forms 1040) for 2011, 2012, and 2013 are being examined. They have decided to appoint Jim Smith, an enrolled agent, to represent them in this matter and any future matters concerning these returns. Jim, who has prepared returns at the same location for years, already has a Centralized Authorization File (CAF) number assigned to him. Mary does not want Jim to sign any agreements on her behalf, but Stan is willing to have Jim do so. They want copies of all notices and written communications sent to Jim. This is the first time Stan and Mary have given power of attorney to anyone. They should each complete a Form 2848 as follows.

Line 1—Taxpayer information. Stan and Mary must each file a separate Form 2848. On his separate Form 2848, Stan enters his name, street address, and social security number in the spaces provided. Mary does likewise on her separate Form 2848.

Line 2—Representative(s). On their separate Forms 2848, Stan and Mary each enters the name and current address of their chosen representative, Jim Smith. Both Stan and Mary want Jim Smith to receive notices and communications concerning the matters identified in line 3, so on their separate Forms 2848, Stan and Mary each checks the box in the first column of line 2. They also enter Mr. Smith's CAF number, his telephone number, and his fax number. Mr. Smith's address, telephone number, and fax number have not changed since the IRS issued his CAF number, so Stan and Mary do not check the boxes in the second column.

Line 3—Tax Matters. On their separate Forms 2848, Stan and Mary each enters "income tax" for the type of matter, "1040" for the form number, and "2011, 2012, and 2013" for the tax years.

Line 4—Specific use not recorded on Centralized Authorization File (CAF). On their separate Forms 2848, Stan and Mary make no entry on this line because they do not want to restrict the use of their powers of attorney to a specific use that is not recorded on the CAF. See Preparation of Form — Helpful Hints , earlier.

Line 5—Acts authorized. Mary wants to sign any agreement that reflects changes to her and Stan's joint 2011, 2012, and 2013 income tax liability, so she writes "Taxpayer must sign any agreement form" on line 5b of her Form 2848. Stan does not wish to restrict the authority of Jim Smith in this regard, so he leaves line 5b of his Form 2848 blank. If either Mary or Stan had chosen, they could have listed other restrictions on line 5b of their separate Forms 2848.

Line 6—Retention/revocation of prior power(s) of attorney. Stan and Mary are each filing their first powers of attorney, so they make no entry on this line. However, if they had filed prior powers of attorney, the filing of this current power would revoke any earlier ones for the same tax matter(s) unless they checked the box on line 6 and attached a copy of the prior power of attorney that they wanted to remain in effect.

If Mary later decides that she can handle the examination on her own, she can revoke her power of attorney even though Stan does not revoke his power of attorney. (See Revocation of Power of Attorney/Withdrawal of Representative , earlier, for the special rules that apply.)

Line 7—Signature of taxpayer. Stan and Mary each signs and dates his or her Form 2848. If a taxpayer does not sign, the IRS cannot accept the form.
Part II—Declaration of Representative. Jim Smith must complete this part of Form 2848. If he does not sign this part, the IRS cannot accept the form.
What Happens to the Power of Attorney When Filed?

A power of attorney will be recognized after it is received, reviewed, and determined by the IRS to contain the required information. However, until a power of attorney is entered on the CAF system, IRS personnel may be unaware of the authority of the person you have named to represent you. Therefore, during this interim period, IRS personnel may request that you or your representative bring a copy to any meeting with the IRS.

This image is too large to be displayed in the current screen. Please click the link to view the image.
Filled-in Form 2848 - Page 1
This image is too large to be displayed in the current screen. Please click the link to view the image.
Filled-in Form 2848 - Page 2
This image is too large to be displayed in the current screen. Please click the link to view the image.
Filled-in Form 2848 - Page 1
This image is too large to be displayed in the current screen. Please click the link to view the image.
Filled-in Form 2848 - Page 2
Processing and Handling

How the power of attorney is processed and handled depends on whether it is a complete or incomplete document.
Incomplete document. If Form 2848 is incomplete, the IRS will attempt to secure the missing information either by writing or telephoning you or your representative. For example, if your signature or signature date is missing, the IRS will contact you. If information concerning your representative is missing and information sufficient to make a contact (such as an address and/or a telephone number) is on the document, the IRS will try to contact your representative.

In either case, the power of attorney is not considered valid until all required information is entered on the document. The individual(s) named as representative(s) will not be recognized to practice before the IRS, on your behalf, until the document is complete and accepted by the IRS.

Complete document. If the power of attorney is complete and valid, the IRS will take action to recognize the representative. In most instances, this includes processing the document on the CAF system. Recording the data on the CAF system enables the IRS to direct copies of mailings to authorized representatives and to readily recognize the scope of authority granted.

Documents not processed on CAF. Specific-use powers of attorney are not processed on the CAF system (see Preparation of Form — Helpful Hints , earlier). For example, a power of attorney that is a one-time or specific-issue grant of authority is not processed on the CAF system. These documents remain with the related case files. In this situation, you should check the box on line 4 of Form 2848. In these situations, the representative should bring a copy of the power of attorney to each meeting with the IRS.

Dealing With the Representative

After a valid power of attorney is filed, the IRS will recognize your representative. However, if it appears the representative is responsible for unreasonably delaying or hindering the prompt disposition of an IRS matter by failing to furnish, after repeated requests, nonprivileged information, the IRS can contact you directly. For example, in most instances in which a power of attorney is recognized, the IRS will contact the representative to set up appointments and to provide lists of required items. However, if the representative is unavailable, does not respond to repeated requests, and does not provide required items (other than items considered privileged), the IRS can bypass your representative and contact you directly.

If a representative engages in conduct described above, the matter can be referred to the Office of Professional Responsibility for consideration of possible disciplinary action.

Notices and other correspondence. If you want to authorize your representative to receive copies of all notices and communications sent to you by the IRS, you must check the box that is provided under the representative's name and address. No more than two representatives may receive copies of notices and communications sent to you by the IRS. Do not check the box if you do not want copies of notices and communications sent to your representative(s).

Note.
Representatives will not receive forms, .s, and other related materials with the correspondence. How To Get Tax Help
Do you need help with a tax issue or preparing your tax return, or do you

need a free . or form?

Preparing and filing your tax return. Find free options to prepare and file your return on IRS.gov or in your local community if you qualify.

• Go to IRS.gov and click on the Filing tab to see your options.

• Enter "Free File" in the search box to use brand name software to prepare and e-file your federal tax return for free.

• Enter "VITA" in the search box, download the free IRS2Go app, or call 1-800-906-9887 to find the nearest Volunteer Income Tax Assistance or Tax Counseling for the Elderly (TCE) location for free tax preparation.

• Enter "TCE" in the search box, download the free IRS2Go app, or call 1-888-227-7669 to find the nearest Tax Counseling for the Elderly location for free tax preparation.

The Volunteer Income Tax Assistance (VITA) program offers free tax help to people who generally make $53,000 or less, persons with disabilities, the elderly, and limited-English-speaking taxpayers who need help preparing their own tax returns. The Tax Counseling for the Elderly (TCE) program offers free tax help for all taxpayers, particularly those who are 60 years of age and older. TCE volunteers specialize in answering questions about pensions and retirement-related issues unique to seniors.

Getting answers to your tax law questions. IRS.gov and IRS2Go are ready when you are—24 hours a day, 7 days a week.

• Enter "ITA" in the search box on IRS.gov for the Interactive Tax Assistant, a tool that will ask you questions on a number of tax law topics and provide answers. You can print the entire interview and the final response.

• Enter "Tax Map" or "Tax Trails" in the search box for detailed information by tax topic.

• Enter "Pub 17" in the search box to get Pub. 17, Your Federal Income Tax for Individuals, which features details on tax-saving opportunities, 2015 tax changes, and thousands of interactive links to help you find answers to your questions.

• Call TeleTax at 1-800-829-4477 for recorded information on a variety of tax topics.

• Access tax law information in your electronic filing software.

• Go to IRS.gov and click on the Help & Resources tab for more information. Tax forms and .s. You can download or print all of the forms and .s you may need on www.irs.gov/formspubs. Otherwise, you can:

• Go to www.irs.gov/orderforms to place an order and have forms mailed to you, or

• Call 1-800-829-3676 to order current-year forms, instructions, .s, and prior-year forms and instructions (limited to 5 years).

You should receive your order within 10 business days.

Where to file your tax return.

• There are many ways to file your return electronically. It's safe, quick and easy. See Preparing and filing your tax return, earlier, for more information.

• See your tax return instructions to determine where to mail your completed paper tax return.

Getting a transcript or copy of a return.

• Go to IRS.gov and click on "Get Transcript of Your Tax Records" under "Tools."

• Download the free IRS2Go app to your smart phone and use it to order transcripts of your tax returns or tax account.

• Call the transcript toll-free line at 1-800-908-9946.

• Mail Form 4506-T or Form 4506T-EZ (both available on IRS.gov).

Using online tools to help prepare your return. Go to IRS.gov and click on the Tools bar to use these and other self-service options.

• The Earned Income Tax Credit Assistant determines if you are eligible for the EIC.

• The First Time Homebuyer Credit Account Look-up tool provides information on your repayments and account balance.

• The Alternative Minimum Tax (AMT) Assistant determines whether you may be subject to AMT.

• The Online EIN Application helps you get an Employer Identification Number.

• The IRS Withholding Calculator estimates the amount you should have withheld from your paycheck for federal income tax purposes.

• The Electronic Filing PIN Request helps to verify your identity when you do not have your prior year AGI or prior year self-selected PIN available.

Understanding identity theft issues.

• Go to www.irs.gov/uac/Identity-Protection for information and videos.

• If your SSN has been lost or stolen or you suspect you are a victim of tax-related identity theft, visit www.irs.gov/identitytheft to learn what steps you should take.

Checking on the status of a refund.

• Go to www.irs.gov/refunds.
• Download the free IRS2Go app to your smart phone and use it to check your refund status.
• Call the automated refund hotline at 1-800-829-1954.

Making a tax payment. You can make electronic payments online, by phone, or from a mobile device. Paying electronically is safe and secure. The IRS uses the latest encryption technology and does not store banking information. It's easy and secure and much quicker than mailing in a check or money order. Go to IRS.gov and click on the Payments tab or the "Pay Your Tax Bill" icon to make a payment using the following options.

• Direct Pay (only if you are an individual who has a checking or savings account).
• Debit or credit card.
• Electronic Federal Tax Payment System.
• Check or money order.

What if I can't pay now? Click on the Payments tab or the "Pay Your Tax Bill" icon on IRS.gov to find more information about these additional options.

• An online payment agreement determines if you are eligible to apply for an installment agreement if you cannot pay your taxes in full today. With the needed information, you can complete the application in about 30 minutes, and get immediate approval.

• An offer in compromise allows you to settle your tax debt for less than the full amount you owe. Use the Offer in Compromise Pre-Qualifier to confirm your eligibility.

Checking the status of an amended return. Go to IRS.gov and click on the Tools tab and then Where's My Amended Return?

Understanding an IRS notice or letter. Enter "Understanding your notice" in the search box on IRS.gov to find additional information about your IRS notice or letter.

Visiting the IRS. Locate the nearest Taxpayer Assistance Center using the

Office Locator tool on IRS.gov. Enter "office locator" in the search box. Or choose the "Contact Us" option on the IRS2Go app and search Local Offices. Before you visit, use the Locator tool to check hours and services available.

Watching IRS videos. The IRS Video portal www.irsvideos.gov contains video and audio presentations on topics of interest to individuals, small businesses, and tax professionals. You'll find video clips of tax topics, archived versions of live panel discussions and Webinars, and audio archives of tax practitioner phone forums.
Getting tax information in other languages. For taxpayers whose native language is not English, we have the following resources available.

1. Taxpayers can find information on IRS.gov in the following languages.
a. Spanish.
b. Chinese.
c. Vietnamese.
d. Korean.
e. Russian.
2. The IRS Taxpayer Assistance Centers provide over-the-phone interpreter service in over 170 languages, and the service is available free to taxpayers.
The Taxpayer Advocate Service Is Here To Help You
What is the Taxpayer Advocate Service?

The Taxpayer Advocate Service (TAS) is an independent organization within the Internal Revenue Service that helps taxpayers and protects taxpayer rights. Our job is to ensure that every taxpayer is treated fairly and that you know and understand your rights under the Taxpayer Bill of Rights.

What Can the Taxpayer Advocate Service Do For You?

We can help you resolve problems that you can't resolve with the IRS. And our service is free. If you qualify for our assistance, you will be assigned to one advocate who will work with you throughout the process and will do everything possible to resolve your issue. TAS can help you if:

• Your problem is causing financial difficulty for you, your family, or your business,
• You face (or your business is facing) an immediate threat of adverse action, or
• You've tried repeatedly to contact the IRS but no one has responded, or the

IRS hasn't responded by the date promised.
How Can You Reach Us?
We have offices in every state, the District of Columbia, and Puerto Rico.
Your local advocate's number is in your local directory and at
www.taxpayeradvocate.irs.gov. You can also call us at 1-877-777-4778.

How Can You Learn About Your Taxpayer Rights? The Taxpayer Bill of
Rights describes ten basic rights that all taxpayers have when dealing with
the IRS. Our Tax Toolkit at www.taxpayeradvocate.irs.gov can help you
understand what these rights mean to you and how they apply. These are your
rights. Know them. Use them.

How Else Does the Taxpayer Advocate Service Help Taxpayers?
TAS works to resolve large-scale problems that affect many taxpayers. If you
know of one of these broad issues, please report it to us at www.irs.gov/sams.
Low Income Taxpayer Clinics

Low Income Taxpayer Clinics (LITCs) serve individuals whose income is
below a certain level and need to resolve tax problems such as audits,
appeals, and tax collection disputes. Some clinics can provide information
about taxpayer rights and responsibilities in different languages for
individuals who speak English as a second language. To find a clinic near
you, visit www.irs.gov/litc or see IRS . 4134, Low Income Taxpayer Clinic
List.

Index
A
Annual Filing Season Program, What's New
Appraisers, Appraisers.
Assistance (see Tax help)
Associations, Corporations, associations, partnerships, and other persons that
are not individuals.
Attorneys, Attorneys.
Authorization letter, Authorization for Special Appearances
C
CAF number, Authorization for Special Appearances
Certified public accountants (CPAs), Certified public accountants (CPAs).
Corporations, Corporations, associations, partnerships, and other persons that
are not individuals.